To: Ton
with appreciation
+ best wishes.
        Michael Fahey
31 March 1996.

The Père Marquette
Lecture in Theology
1996

Orthodox and Catholic Sister Churches:
East is West and West is East

Michael A Fahey, s.j.
Dean of Theology
University of St. Michael's College, Toronto

MARQUETTE
UNIVERSITY

PRESS

Library of Congress Cataloguing-in-Publication Data

Fahey, Michael A. (Michael Andrew), 1933-
  Orthodox and Catholic sister churches : East is West and
West is East / Michael A. Fahey, S.J.
    p. cm. — (The Père Marquette lecture in theology ; 1996)
    Includes bibliographical references.
    ISBN 0-87462-576-9 (cloth)
    1. Orthodox Eastern Church—Relations—Catholic Church.
  2. Catholic Church—Relations—Orthodox Eastern Church.
  I. Title. II. Series.
  BX324.3.F34 1996
  280' .2—dc20   96-4522

Copyright © 1996
Marquette University Press
Milwaukee WI 53201-1881

Manufactured in the United States of America

Marquette University Press
MILWAUKEE

The Association of Jesuit University Presses

FOREWORD

The annual Père Marquette Lecture in Theology commemorates the missions and explorations of Père Jacques Marquette, S.J. (1637-75). The 1996 lecture is the twenty-seventh in the series begun in 1969 under the auspices of the Marquette University Department of Theology.

The Joseph A. Auchter Family Endowment Fund has endowed the lecture series. Joseph Auchter (1894-1986), a native of Milwaukee, was a banking and paper industry executive and a long-time supporter of education. The fund was established by his children as a memorial to him.

MICHAEL A. FAHEY, S.J.

Michael A. Fahey, S.J., was born in Fremont, Ohio, in 1933, but grew up in Norwalk, Connecticut, where he attended elementary schools. He studied at the Jesuit-run Fairfield College Preparatory School and in 1951 entered the New England Province of the Society of Jesus. He majored in classics at Boston College and from 1955 to 1958 studied philosophy at the University of Louvain (Facultés St. Albert), Belgium. After teaching high school for two years at Fairfield Prep, he did graduate studies in Romance Languages and Literature at Fordham University, New

York City, where he received an M.A. in 1961. He
obtained a licentiate in theology from the Weston
School of Theology (1965) and was ordained in 1964.
He did post-graduate studies in ascetical theology in
Carinthia, Austria, 1965-66 and graduate studies in
historical theology at the University of Tübingen,
Germany, where he obtained the doctorate in theology
(Dr. theol.) in 1970. He taught at the Weston Jesuit
School of Theology in Cambridge, Massachusetts,
from 1970-1975. He was professor of systematic
theology in the Department of Theological Studies at
Concordia University, Montreal, from 1976-1986; in
1985 he was visiting professor at Rome's Pontificio
Istituto Orientale (Institute of Eastern Christian Studies), part of the Gregorian University consortium. He
is currently completing his tenth year as Dean of the
Faculty of Theology, at the University of St. Michael's
College, Toronto, part of the Toronto School of Theology.

Fr. Fahey has lectured and travelled widely. His
research focuses especially on historical and doctrinal
issues that have separated the Christian churches, especially divisions between the Christian East and West.
Besides major articles in theological journals and col-
laborative volumes devoted to various topics concern-
ing church unity, he has published several books,
including *Cyprian and the Bible: A Study in Third-
Century Exegesis*; and *Trinitarian Theology East and
West; Catholic Perspectives on Baptism, Eucharist, and
Ministry*; "Church" in *Systematic Theology: Roman*

Catholic Perspectives, ed. F.S. Fiorenza and J. Galvin (Minneapolis: Fortress, 1992); and *Ecumenism* (1993). He has collaborated in several research projects with the Catholic Theological Society of America. He has also translated a series of theological essays by Karl Rahner.

In a number of countries he has observed various attempts at church unity and the inter-relationship of culture and religious beliefs. He has served as a consultant for the Canadian Centre for Ecumenism in Montreal and has served for over 25 years as Executive Secretary of the Orthodox/Roman Catholic Consultation in the United States sponsored by the Bishops' Committee in Ecumenical and Interreligious Affairs of the USCC. He is also past president of the Catholic Theological Society of America. He is now serving a five-year appointment as Editor in Chief of the journal of *Theological Studies*.

Michel René Barnes

ORTHODOX AND CATHOLIC
SISTER CHURCHES:
EAST IS WEST AND
WEST IS EAST

**Dedicated to the memory of
Yves Congar, O.P. (1904-1995)**

Rudyard Kipling, the famous English poet and observer of India's cultural distinctiveness, expressed his oft-cited convictions about the irreconcilable differences between Britain and the Indian subcontinent in his "The Ballad of East and West":

Oh, East is East, and West is West,
  and never the twain shall meet,
Till Earth and Sky stand presently
  at God's great Judgment Seat;
But there is neither East nor West,
  Border, nor Breed, nor Birth,
When two strong men stand face to face,
  though they come from the ends of the earth!

As regards the two major ecclesial heritages, Rome and Byzantium, however, such a neat division into

two parts is no longer meaningful. These two enti-
ties were better described first by Yves Congar and
later by Pope Paul VI as the "two lungs" of Christianity, the one evangelized out of the Western
Mediterranean city of Rome, and the other evangelized from the Eastern Mediterranean metropolis of
Byzantium or Constantinople. Today the two are so
intertwined that boundaries are down. Not only is
this true geographically — an "Eastern" church may
grace a block in Brooklyn, and a "Western" church
may be tucked away in a Moscow suburb — but
culturally and theologically too the two churches
interact intimately even when remaining in their
"traditional" loci such as the Phanar or the Vatican.
What shall we call them: Latin and Greek, Roman
and Byzantine, papal and synodal, centralist and
autocephalous? All these differentiations are inad-
equate, all the more so inasmuch as they omit two
other Western Asian church communities: the Ancient Oriental Orthodox churches (Armenian,
Coptic, Ethiopian, Syrian and Malankaran) and the
Assyrian Church of the East, once inappropriately
labeled the "Nestorians."[1]

In my twenty-six years of close collaboration
with Christians of various Eastern churches, I have
learned much about the ecclesial unity and diversity
existing among these churches formed originally
within the cultural ambit of Byzantium or the Le-
vant but now also firmly established outside the
Eastern Mediterranean. Eastern churches are very

much alive far beyond the "East," and are deeply rooted in the West: the United States, Canada, Australia, South America, and elsewhere.

Through the goodness of God, the estrangement between Eastern and Western Christianity that the late Dominican Father Yves Congar described in his pioneering work *After Nine Hundred Years*,[2] has now to a great extent, after 942 years, been healed if not officially acknowledged. I wish to describe some of the stages in that healing and their causes, as well as certain neuralgic issues that still weaken full visible communion between the two largest groups of Christian believers: Catholics and Orthodox.

When the Second Vatican Council published *Unitatis redintegratio*, its Decree on Ecumenism, on November 21, 1964, Roman Catholics finally began to catch up with the Orthodox, Anglicans, and Protestants in efforts to restore full visible communion among the Christian communities. Prior to that, as is well known, Catholics practiced a sort of "Prodigal Son" model of ecumenism. Once you were willing to admit "I have sinned against you" Catholics would welcome the sinners back into the "true church."[3] Looked at with a keen historical eye, efforts by Catholics in this century to bring to fruition the prayer of Jesus "that all may be one" were by far widely anticipated by other Christians, not the least of whom were the Orthodox led by Joachim III, Ecumenical Patriarch of Constantinople, in his early and much-heralded 1902 encyclical.[4]

At Vatican II (1962-1965), because of the serious preparatory work of Eastern and Western historians and theologians as well as the efforts of some Eastern Catholic hierarchs, the Church of Rome was finally able to admit its past failures in not respecting the traditions of the Eastern churches. In its Decree on Eastern Catholic Churches (*Orientalium ecclesiarum*) and the Decree on Ecumenism (*Unitatis redintegratio*) some astounding statements about Eastern Christianity occur. In the second decree it was noted that: "Similarly it must not be forgotten that from the beginning the churches of the East have had a treasury from which the Western church has drawn extensively — in liturgical practice, spiritual tradition and canon law. Nor must we undervalue the fact that it was the ecumenical councils held in the East that defined the basic dogmas of the Christian faith, on the Trinity and on the Word of God, who took flesh of the Virgin Mary." (no. 14)[5] Catholics were asked "...to give due consideration to this special feature of the origin and growth of the Eastern churches, and to the character of the relations which obtained between them and the Roman See before separation and to learn to give weight to all these factors." (no. 14) That document also praised the strong liturgical life of the Eastern churches and stated that "these churches, though separated from us, yet possess true sacraments, above all, by apostolic succession, the priesthood and the Eucharist, whereby they are still linked with us in closest intimacy." (no. 15) It continued stating that "from the earliest times the Eastern churches followed their own disciplines, which were sanctioned by the approval of the fathers of the church and of synods, even of ecumenical councils. Far from being an obstacle to the Church's unity, a certain diversity of customs and observances only adds to her beauty and is of great help in carrying out her mission." The text continued by stating that these churches "have the right to govern themselves according to the disciplines proper to themselves" (no. 16). It also stressed that there is a legitimate variety in theological expression of doctrine (no. 17) and finally prayed for the removal of the wall dividing the Eastern and Western Church (no. 18).

In the previous decree, *Orientalium ecclesiarum,* it was stated that "History, traditions and very many ecclesiastical institutions bear witness to what extent the Eastern churches have merited well of the whole church." The Council "not only bestows due esteem and rightful praise on this ecclesiastical and spiritual heritage but firmly regards it as the heritage of the whole church of Christ." (no. 5)

These texts express what it is that the Roman Catholic community and other Christian churches have been receiving and hope to receive from the Orthodox and Eastern Catholic churches. As in other texts of Vatican II, one might have hoped for a more forthright admission of guilt by Catholics, in this case regarding the often troubled history of relationship between the Eastern and Western churches. Still, although the disedifying incidents regarding Rome's interference in the affairs of the Eastern churches are not specifically enumerated, they are alluded to in the Decree on Ecumenism which, after citing 1 Jn 1:10 ("If we say that we have not sinned"...), goes on to state: "The words of St. John hold good about sins against unity...so we humbly beg pardon of God and of our separated sisters and brothers, just as we forgive them that trespass against us." (no. 7)

Historians and specifically biographers of John XXIII, pope from 1958 to 1963, are now beginning to recognize the indirect impact that Eastern Orthodoxy had on that pope's dream of convening a general synod for Catholics. During the nineteen years that the future Pope John XXIII served as apostolic nuncio, first in the predominantly Orthodox Bulgaria (1925-1935) and then in Turkey and Greece (1935-1944), he came to know and love the people and clergy of the Orthodox churches more closely than any of the modern-day popes. Long before Rome's gestures of the 1960s, Angelo Roncalli as early as the 1930s had undertaken regular visits to the Ecumenical Patriarch of Constantinople.

The reason why the Eastern and Western Christians are committed to dialogue now is ultimately the fruit of God's reconciling grace which led to a change of heart bringing the ecumenical patriarchs and the popes to find ways to eliminate estrangement. We recall the historic meeting in 1964 of Ecumenical Patriarch Athenagoras and Pope Paul VI in Jerusalem's Gethsemane near the Mount of Olives. Subsequent establishment of regular mutual visits and shared prayer services, as we shall see, followed from this historic initiative.

The History of the Expression "Sister Churches"

Part of the shift came from an understanding that these two lungs form "sister churches." This perception that separate churches could be sisters is already hinted at in the New Testament. It has been lived in the churches long before the Council of Nicaea, and right up to today has been articulated in practices found in 20th century Catholic and Orthodox churches, as well as in international and national ecumenical consultations. Let us draw upon some recent studies on the origin of this phrase as background to our reflections.[6]

The New Testament letter, 2 John, in verse 13 concludes with a salutation sending greetings to another Christian community described as "sister." The expression as such, it is true, does not occur elsewhere in the New Testament corpus. However, in the closing sections of 1 Pet 5:13, Rom 16:16 and 1 Cor 16:19-20 there are similar greetings to a church, although the exact word sister is not used. What is frequent in the New Testament is the expression "brother(s)" (which we now appropri-

ately translate as "brothers and sisters") to denote
fellow Christians. This is not just a stereotypical
polite formula but a term with sacramental over-
tones, since other believers and their churches are
seen as sharers in salvation achieved by Jesus Christ
and effecting communion in the Holy Spirit.

Valuable historical studies over the last decades
on the notion *koinonia* or *communio* have shown
that local churches had an acute sense that they,
despite notable diversity of practices among them,
belonged to a network of churches forming together
"the Church of God." These sibling Christian communities developed an acute sense of sharing throughout pre-Nicene Christianity. The clear implication
is that they were part of a family, we would say today,
they considered themselves to be "sister churches."
We have considerable historical witnesses to at least
six practices whereby local churches fostered solidar-
ity and communion among diverse communities:
(a) prayers for one another at eucharistic celebrations and sharing eucharistic bread between churches;
(b) installing new bishops by inviting bishops from
neighboring churches to ordain them; (c) convoking
regional synods or councils to solve disciplinary and
doctrinal issues; (d) exchanging and circulating letters on a variety of matters including the results of
episcopal elections, eucharistic and baptismal practices, or testifying to the orthodoxy of a traveling
Christian who sought hospitality; (e) accepting attempts at coordination by the bishop of Rome at

least among the Western churches; and (f) with the conversion of Constantine, acquiescing to direct interventions by the Roman Emperor in the administrative life of the church.[7]

The publication *Tomos Agapis,* a collection of documents between the Vatican and the Phanar 1958-1970 (translated and expanded to the year 1984 by E.J. Stormon, S.J., *Towards the Healing of Schism: The Sees of Rome and Constantinople*), provides a number of examples of the use of the expression in more recent times. Patriarch Athenagoras referred to the Church of Rome as a "sister Church" in a letter addressed to Cardinal Bea on April 12, 1962, writing: "What you have to say in general terms about your desire for the *rapprochement* of the sister Churches and the restoration of unity in the Church moved us deeply, as it was bound to do, given the fact that we have repeatedly manifested our own readiness to do all in our power to contribute to this restoration." (*Tomos Agapis* [*TA*] no. 10; Stormon, p. 35). The usage is all the more remarkable inasmuch as Cardinal Bea had not used the term himself.

Shortly after his election to the papacy, Pope Paul VI wrote a handwritten letter to Patriarch Athenagoras on Sept. 20, 1963 (*TA* no. 33). Athenagoras published a Greek translation of this in his patriarchal bulletin *Apostolos Andreas* (Nov. 6, 1963) and giving it the title "The two sister-churches." The term is also found in Patriarch Athenagoras' telegram of March 27, 1964 to Paul VI (*TA* no. 58); in a letter to the pope on May 19, 1964 (*TA* no. 65), and in an allocution of Metropolitan Meliton to Paul VI February 16, 1965 (*TA* no. 87).

The reason why East and West are actively promoting the restoration of full communion lies in their response to God's graces promoting closer unity among Christians. The use of the term "sister Churches" has helped contribute to that change of heart in the two churches whereby they are committed to eliminating estrangement. A visual expression of this came in 1964 through the historic visit of Pope Paul VI to Jerusalem. As we noted, they exchanged there an historic embrace symbolizing the commitment of our churches to work for reunion. The following year, on December 7, 1965, there occurred the mutual lifting and banishing into oblivion the anathemas between Constantinople and Rome dating back to the year A.D. 1054. Pope Paul visited Athenagoras in Istanbul in 1967 and there was an exchange of letters in 1971 about a "common sacramental cup" to which they both aspire.

This change of heart and choice of vocabulary is reflected in conciliar and patriarchal/papal documents. Vatican II's Decree on Ecumenism *Unitatis redintegratio* (1964) stated that:

> Among other matters of moment, it is a pleasure for this synod to remind everyone that there exist in the East many particular or local churches, among which the patriarchal churches hold first place, and many of which are proud to trace their origins back to the apostles them-

selves. Hence a matter of primary concern and care among the Easterns has been, and still is, to preserve the family ties of common faith and charity which ought to exist between local churches, as between sisters [*inter ecclesias locales, ut inter sorores, vigere debent*]." (no. 14)

Also on the Catholic side the term was used on November 22, 1965 by Cardinal Willebrands when with a papal commission he had been charged to prepare the draft formulation for the lifting of the 1054 anathemas (*TA* no. 123). The actual joint declaration removing the anathemas (*TA* no. 127) dated December 7, 1965, does not use the expression but the idea is present.

But a text par excellence that enshrines Roman Catholic use of the term sister churches for the Orthodox is Paul VI's brief *Anno ineunte*, of July 25, 1967 (*TA* no. 176, Stormon, pp. 161-62) which states:

> In each local Church this mystery of divine love is enacted, and surely this is the ground of the traditional and very beautiful expression "sister churches," which local churches were fond of applying to one another. (Cf. Decree, *Unitatis Redintegratio*, 14). For centuries we lived this life of "sister churches," and together held the Ecumenical Councils which guarded the deposit of faith against all corruption. And now, after a long period of division and mutual misunderstanding, the Lord is enabling us to discover ourselves as "sister churches" once more, in spite of the obstacles which were once raised between us. In the light of Christ we see how urgent is the need of surmounting these ob-

stacles in order to succeed in bringing to its fullness and perfection the already very rich communion which exists between us.

Other texts use the same expression Paul VI (*TA* no. 269). There are many allusions to the brotherly relationship of Peter and Andrew (*TA*, pp. 103, 378, 584, 590). In fact Peter and Andrew become metaphorical expressions for the Roman and Byzantine churches as is seen in the speech of Dec. 28, 1963, delivered at the Vatican by Metropolitan Athenagoras of Thyateira: "Peter and Andrew were brothers. For centuries they were not on speaking terms, but now here they are both expressing a desire to meet and talk to one another." (*TA* no. 44; Stormon p. 59).

A visual expression of this same reality also occurred on December 14, 1975, when Metropolitan Meliton, personal representative of the Ecumenical Patriarch Dimitrios I, announced to Pope Paul VI in the Sistine Chapel the Pan-Orthodox decision to establish a special inter-Orthodox theological commission, the purpose of which was to prepare, for the Orthodox side, formal theological dialogue with Roman Catholics. Pope Paul greeted the news with the stunning gesture of falling to his knees and kissing the feet of Metropolitan Meliton, who conveyed the good news, thereby evoking St. Paul's words citing Isaiah in Rom 10:15: "How beautiful are the feet of those who preach the good news!" That gesture of reconciliation and joy, together with Paul's historic amplexus of Patriarch Athenagoras in January 1964 during his visit to

Jerusalem, may well be regarded as the high points of Pope Paul's pontificate. Ecumenical Patriarch Dimitrios I later said of that gesture: "Paul VI a dépassé la papauté [Paul VI has transcended the papacy]."

Being sister churches is founded on the reality of our common status as children of the same Father, in Jesus Christ, and sharing in the communion of the Holy Spirit preeminently through baptism. This status is founded not only in baptism, but also in the priesthood, in apostolic succession, and in the Eucharist all of which make a church a true church.

The use of the term especially in modern times allows us confidently to assert with Yves Congar at least three affirmations.[8] They are:

1) As far as Orthodox and Roman Catholics are concerned there is only one Church. However, this Church is a Church divided, but not in the sense that one might say that on one side there is the Church and on the other side a group which is not the Church. Father Congar as early as 1952 was using the image that the Church exists with two lungs, one of the West one of the East, an image than Pope John Paul II later borrowed on several occasions. (See the Pope's allocution to the Roman Curia, June 28, 1980; and his allocution to representatives of other churches, Paris, May 31, 1980 [cf. *Service d'information* no. 44 (1980) pp. 86 and 94]).

2) The same Church exists in two distinctive traditions.

3) The substance of the faith and the reality of
the sacraments in the Orthodox Church and in the
Roman Catholic Church rest on the apostolicity of the
Church. Catholics recognize that the Orthodox Church
is not a daughter church but truly a sister church.

It is true that Paul VI applied the term "sister
church" in a particular sense to the Anglican Communion on the occasion of the Canonization of the
Forty Martyrs of England and Wales, St. Peter's
Basilica, October 25, 1970. The text in question
reads:

> There will be no seeking to lessen the legitimate
> prestige and the worthy patrimony of piety and
> usage proper to the Anglican Church when the
> Roman Catholic Church—this humble 'Ser-
> vant of the servants of God'—is able to embrace
> her ever beloved sister in the one authentic
> communion of the family of Christ: a commun-
> ion of origin and of faith, a communion of
> priesthood and of rule, a communion of saints
> in the freedom of love of the spirit of Jesus.[9]

But this text needs to be read carefully noting
that Paul VI does not state that the two churches are
de facto "sisters" at the present time. It speaks of a
future event. His remark should not distract from
the fact that for centuries Rome and Byzantium have
considered each other sister churches.

Sisters Yes, But Identical Twins No

My own association with Eastern churches and
theology over the last decades has helped me under-

stand that whereas our two ecclesial traditions allow us to recognize one another as sisters we are certainly not identical twins. *Vive la différence!* Eastern Christianity's valuable contributions to our worldwide living as Church can assist Roman Catholics by teaching them its specific understanding of: (a) the importance of the local or particular church, and (b) the need for conciliarity or sobornicity at every level of ecclesial life.

(a) Regarding the centrality of the local or particular church this is what Catholics need to learn from the Eastern churches:

(1) A valuable point of departure for understanding the Church is the Ignatian vision of the local church: the faithful as church come together *epi to auto* (1 Cor 11:17, 20; 14:23, 26), they become the body of Christ in the eucharist, and the bishop signifies this unity, summing up the local church in himself but governing in synodal fashion.

(2) The eucharistic assembly under the presidency of the bishop is completely church in all its fullness, a complete church even if not the total Church; the local church is not just a part of the Church so that the church that dwells in Corinth has the same fullness as the church in Jerusalem, Antioch, or Rome.

(3) This status of all the local churches implies the essential unity and equality of all bishops.

(4) This equality of local churches and of bishops does not mean uniformity, just as unity of essence cannot exclude plurality of unique hypostases.

Each local church is unique. Among them some may "preside in love," some may express more completely and perfectly the shared faith. Many factors may have contributed to a church's potential for presiding: antiquity, presumed apostolicity of foundation, martyrdom, geopolitical advantages, size, wealth. In contemporary Eastern Christian church life there are three types of episcopal primacy: (a) that of the regional primacy of a metropolitan-archbishop who presides within the synod of bishops of a particular geographical region; (b) the primacy of the head of an autocephalous church; and (c) the unique and distinctive primacy of the patriarch of Constantinople who is recognized as the ecumenical patriarch.

Catholic ecclesiology in the West, especially since the Council of Trent but in fact much earlier, has operated out of a "two-tiered" model of church: the diocese (an *ecclesia particularis*) and, without intermediary structure, the universal church.[10] Hence in this two-deckered vision there is little room for the autocephalous or autonomous church. This narrower Western vision of Church resulted from the effects of the estrangement between East and West, which culminated in 1054 but which in fact originated much earlier. In the Catholic West, papal and patriarchal jurisdictions merged into one office, thus producing in the mind of the Roman church the conviction that it presided over the universal Church. This historical process may explain in part why today the Vatican has so much difficulty in accepting the magisterial competence of episcopal conferences over many matters, and why the Vatican's central administration holds on firmly to supervising the process by which bishops are appointed in every country. Such a two-tiered ecclesiology has undesirable implications, especially when it restricts the diocesan bishop's responsibilities principally to the promulgation of the theological opinions or the governing priorities of the incumbent pope.

The West needs to reappropriate some form of the three-tiered church in which the local or particular church would be seen to be an intermediate ecclesial unit. Episcopal conferences should be seen not primarily as a convening of bishops but of churches represented by bishops. Whether an episcopal conference or some other form of intermediate ecclesial governance should be assigned a similar role as that of the historic synodal institutions of the past is a question that needs discussion. But the present centralist situation in the Roman Catholic Church certainly promotes tension and poses serious obstacles to the re-establishment of Rome's full visible communion with the churches of the East.

(b) Regarding the Eastern understanding of conciliarity or synodality:

My conviction expressed here is that governance in the churches of the Christian East, for all the problems associated with caesaro-papism, triumphalism, ethnocentrism, and immobilism, has preserved a profound understanding of the Church's conciliarity or its synodal (sometimes called synodical) character.[11] Not every church has achieved this same level of preservation. Indeed I would argue that the state of unrest in Roman Catholicism is centered upon two issues: first, the governing role to be assigned to national episcopal conferences; and secondly, ways to preserve national or cultural distinctiveness in a church ever subject to centralist models of church administration. This tension, in my judgment, comes from a widespread reduction in Catholicism of appropriate forms of synodal structures that are not just a luxury but are indispensable.

First some linguistic reflections on the word "synod" and "conciliar." The Greek language uses the word *synodos* in a double function to describe what the Latin Church calls either a *concilium* or a *synodus*.[12] In ecclesiastical Greek, *synodos* is closely allied to the biblical term *ekklesia* as well as having roots in pre-Christian Jewish religious practices.[13] In the consciousness of today's Eastern Christians, including Eastern Catholics in full communion with the Roman church (at least those who have not lost their ecclesial distinctiveness through Romanization), the Church must always exist synodically or in synod if it is to remain faithful to its charter. In the Byzantine East, because of this dual meaning of "synod," the term does not connote, as it frequently does in the West, only an institution or event that is local or relatively minor. Nor does the synodal or conciliar constitute a reality restricted to bishops or confined solely to gatherings, be they ecumenical, provincial, patriarchal. Synodality, conciliarity or sobornicity (to use the Slavic equivalent) is a characteristic expected to pervade every dimension of ecclesial life. Eastern theologians state that the Church expresses communion in Christ through its synodal character. Hence, for Eastern churches, any ecclesial practice that is not conciliar or synodal is judged to be defective.

Theologians and canonists of the East stress that the synodal expression of ecclesial life should be found in every act of communion among all the members of the Body of Christ. The Church's "order" (*taxis*) is an organic expression of the very nature of the Church. Whereas the Roman church in recent times has often extolled "communion" ecclesiology, the Eastern Orthodox and Eastern Catholics prefer to speak of the Church's conciliarity or its "sobornicity." Eastern Christians are uneasy about the Roman church not only because of how papal prerogatives are perceived, but because it is seen to neglect true conciliarity. A typical judgment on this is the comment of the late Romanian Orthodox theologian, Dumitru Staniloae:

> Sobornicity is distinguished from an undifferentiated unity by being of a special kind, the unity of communion. The Roman Catholic Church has lost this sense of catholicity as communion, for the doctrine of papal primacy and the ecclesiastical magisterium make impos-

sible the communion of all the members of the
Church in all things. The Roman Catholic
Church remains content with the unity which
characterizes a body under command, and it has
replaced the unity of communion (catholicity
or sobornicity properly so-called) with the uni-
versality in the sense of geographical exten-
sion.[14]

One way in which the synodal life of the Church
for Eastern Christians is expressed is by the patriarchs and heads of the various autocephalous churches
who give expression to the mutual communion
among their particular churches. But synodal expression is also manifested, it is judged, in every act
of communion between a metropolitan and other
bishops in his province, between a bishop and his
presbyterate (the priests in his jurisdiction), as well
as between presbyter and faithful in a particular
parish, and finally even among the faithful themselves. As the Orthodox Metropolitan of Pergamon,
the theologian John D. Zizioulas, stressed at the
1988 symposium on episcopal conferences held in
Salamanca: "Bishops are not to be understood as
individuals but as heads of communities."[15] At every
level, the Church is expected to function as a harmo-
nious symphony of believers who have been gath-
ered in Christ upon whom the Holy Spirit rests.
Conciliarity seeks to fashion ecclesiastical life in a
way that will express the Church's nature and distinctiveness. This synodal way of life is intended to
signify how human beings are called by God's grace

to collaborate in the work of redemption and the preservation of the apostolic tradition.

Ecclesiologists have particularly studied the synodal nature of the Church as expressed in the patriarchal "permanent synod" (*synodos endemousa*).[16] It is notable that only in the twelfth century was the institution of a permanent synod in the church of Rome replaced by the consistory of cardinals. Eastern theologians ask that the See of Rome recognize as legitimate the synodal structures of the East especially in those regions where historically Rome did not exercise patriarchal jurisdiction. They also expect Rome to admit the contingent character of Vatican I's formulations about papal primacy and infallibility.

How a *synodos endemousa* or a "permanent synod" operates in the life of a patriarchate can be illustrated by noting the genesis of several encyclical letters regarding the ecumenical movement published in this century by Constantinople. The 1902 encyclical on ecumenism, identified as "A Patriarchal and Synodal Encyclical," was signed and published by the Ecumenical Patriarch Joachim II and eleven other members of the synod. Likewise the follow-up document dating from 1904 which summarizes responses of the local Orthodox churches to the preceding encyclical is signed by the Ecumenical Patriarch and eleven metropolitans of the patriarchate. But surprisingly for Western Catholics the next notable encyclical from the Patriarchate of

Constantinople on church unity, issued in January 1920, was promulgated during a vacancy in the Ecumenical Patriarchate (*sede vacante*) and was signed only by the *locum tenens* and members of the synod. Such a procedure would be inconceivable in the Roman Church.

The Eastern churches recognize that throughout history there has been a variety of synodal structures shaped by time and circumstances. These include regional, general, provincial, ecumenical synods, as well as the permanent patriarchal synod that collaborates in the administration of a patriarchate or of an autocephalous church. Such a patriarchal synod is "permanent" (*endemousa*) in the sense that its bishop members, normally located in Constantinople, can be conveniently convened by the Patriarch.

From early centuries, synods became vehicles for electing bishops and for reaching agreements. In a real sense, the ecclesiological and dogmatic justification for these permanent synods is the sacrament of order. The origins of the so-called *endemousa* synod are rooted in the practice of having the Patriarch of Constantinople summon the bishops residing in the capital city at the time (*endemountes*) to ponder serious issues. Its historical roots, which go back to Constantinople I (A.D. 381) are linked to convening bishops in the capital in order to elect a bishop. This kind of synod grew in importance especially in the eighth century, until it became a permanent institution in the Byzantine Church. It grew to concern itself with doctrinal disputes, legislative matters and disciplinary questions and came to exceed the limited role of the provincial synod. It did not require the elaborate preparations for an ecumenical synod.

In praising the preservation of a sense of synodality in the Eastern churches, I do not mean to imply that they are always faithful to these convictions. Individual church leaders may neglect what in their heart of hearts they know to be appropriate procedures. Political or social crises such as long-term domination by Islam or Soviet communism may led to autocratic decision making, but this is not what is understood as fitting.

The Fruits of the Joint International Consultation

Before commenting on the future theological tasks facing our two sister churches, let me review briefly the remarkable achievements of the joint International Theological Consultation set up by the Orthodox and Catholics. The change in ecumenical climate through study and symbolic actions led to the establishment of the Commission which has already held a series of fruitful plenary sessions and a host of meetings of sub-commissions. Plenary sessions have taken place in Patmos/Rhodes (May 28 to June 4, 1980), in Munich (June 30 to July 6, 1982), in Crete (May 30 to June 8, 1984), in Bari,

Italy (May 28 to June 7, 1986 & June 9 to 16, 1987), in New Valamo, Finland (June 19 to 27, 1988), in Munich-Freising (June 6 to 15, 1990) and most recently in Balamand, Lebanon (June 17 to 24, 1993). Four historic agreed statements have been published to date: "The Mystery of the Church and of the Eucharist in the Light of the Mystery of the Blessed Trinity" (Munich, July 6, 1982); "Faith, Sacraments and the Unity of the Church" (Bari, August 1, 1987); "The Sacrament of Order in the Sacramental Structure of the Church with Particular Reference to the Importance of Apostolic Succession for the Sanctification and Unity of the People of God" (New Valamo, June 26, 1988); "Uniatism, Method of Union of the Past, and the Present Search for Full Communion" (Balamand, Lebanon, June 23, 1993). The agenda item for future meetings will focus next on the topic: "The Ecclesiological and Canonical Consequences of the Sacramental Structure of the Church: Conciliarity and Authority in the Church."[17]

From these agreed statements it is clear that our churches are committed to presenting their sacramental beliefs in theological language that avoids both Western Scholastic or Eastern Palamite categories. The new sacramental theology being jointly formulated attempts for the most part to draw upon Scriptural, liturgical and patristic language. The ascetical-like practice of a mutual renunciation of other language dear to our theological traditions is praiseworthy. Few Western theologians appreciate however that since the Eastern churches did not pass through the same secular experiences Westerners identify as the Renaissance, the Reformation, or the Enlightenment, the East has often preserved certain ancient thought patterns and paradigms no longer considered pertinent in the West.

The consensus statements assert that the churches of Rome and of the Eastern Orthodox recognize as same their basic creedal affirmations on the sacraments, despite the fact that the Orthodox are often puzzled, troubled, and unwilling to imitate some practices of Rome, especially in regard to the sacraments of initiation.

Allow me to share with you some specific reflections about several of these international texts. In the case of the Munich document, the first official joint statement of East and West since the Council of Florence (1431-1445), which shows the intimate relationship between Church and Eucharist, one can hail several features: that Orthodox and Catholics speak with unanimity on a matter of such importance; that the text recognizes the central role of the Holy Spirit in the economy of salvation and offers a strong trinitarian account of the doctrine of the Church; that its theology of eucharistic celebration affirms the centrality of both the anamnesis and the epiclesis; and that the text affirms the importance of conciliarity in every aspect of church life.

Still, besides the positive achievements there are some problems in the text's formulations. As is also true about the next two published agreed statements (Bari and New Valamo), their architects seem unclear about their intended audience. Who exactly is being addressed? Is it the average believer? Then certainly the language is too obscure, in fact even most professional theologians would be mystified by much of the language. Furthermore, the strongly affirmed eucharistic ecclesiology in the document places so much stress on the centrality of the eucharist that the importance of baptism seems eclipsed. The emphasis on the office of *episkopos* somewhat overshadows the historic office of the *presbyteros*. Little use is made by the text's drafters of the valuable insights drawn from a responsible use of the historico-critical method in both biblical and patristic data, as, for instance, the growth and legitimate changes in the office of episcopate. Finally, although there is some minimal mention of the social mission of the Church connected to the celebration of the Eucharist, this dimension is generally understated.

In the Bari text on faith and the sacraments one continues to find a conscious effort to avoid polemical and late medieval Western Scholastic terminology, but surprisingly Scripture is cited much too sparingly. The text effectively relates local church to church universal especially where it says: "[these local churches] have used varied formulas and different languages which, according to the genius of different cultures, bring into relief particular aspects and implications of the unique salvation event" (no. 10). But there is need for greater precision in the way that the text tries to describe the relationship of Jesus Christ, the Logos, to the Holy Spirit. Once again the drafters should have given closer attention to historical developments in the liturgy of Christian initiation.

In the New Valamo text on the sacrament of orders once again one is led to ask: to whom is this text addressed? The language is so specialized that few except for experts will understand its vocabulary or allusions. By now a new problem begins to emerge. Regretfully the texts reflect little cognizance of the fact that in the Christian churches a number of bilateral conversations are underway that have been wrestling with these very same issues. Could not the drafters have drawn upon some of the general conclusions that have been arrived at, conclusions that are not unique to Western theologians? For instance, had the Valamo text profited from the bilateral and multilateral agreements on ministry in dialogues which have even used Orthodox and Catholic theologians it would have been slow to have understood the New Testament concept *diakonia* (service) to refer exclusively to the ministry of the ordained. The Valamo text is not very successful in how it attempts to explain the relationships: Christ—the Twelve—the New Testament apostles—and, the successors to apostles. The document even fails to differentiate where appropriate the New Testament distinction between "the Twelve" and "apostle(s)." Valamo does not address the fact that at least sometimes Paul uses the terms *episkopos* and *presbyteros* interchangeably. Valamo has useful remarks about "the synodal character of episcopal activity" (no. 53) as well as a succinct but comprehensive description of ecumenical councils: "In ecumenical councils, convened in the Holy Spirit at times of crisis, bishops of the church, with supreme authority, decided together about the faith and issued canons to affirm the tradition of the apostles in historic circumstances which directly threatened the faith, unity and sanctifying work of the whole people of God, and put at risk the very existence of the Church and its fidelity to its founder, Jesus Christ." (no. 54). But it does not refer to the unfinished business relating to primacy in the church and particularly to the extent of primacy of the Bishop of Rome, an issue that is simply said to be "a question which constitutes a serious divergence among us and which will be discussed in the future."

Finally in the Balamand text published on "Uniatism, Method of Union of the Past, and the Present Search for Full Communion" the Commission noted that the normal progression of the international dialogue had been set aside so that immediate attention might be given to the question called "Uniatism" occasioned specifically by events that had recently occurred in the former Soviet Union and elsewhere in Eastern Europe. The agreed statement asserts that "what Christ has entrusted to his Church—profession of apostolic faith, participation in the same sacraments, above all the one priesthood celebrating the one sacrifice of Christ, the apostolic succession of bishops - cannot be considered the exclusive right of one of our Churches." (no. 13). The text continues: "It is in this perspective that the Catholic Churches and the Orthodox Churches recognize each other as Sister Churches, responsible together for maintaining the Church of God in what concerns unity." (no. 14). "Pastoral activity in the Catholic Church, Latin as well as Oriental, no longer aims at having the faithful of one Church pass over to the other; that is to say, it no longer aims at proselytizing among the Orthodox." (no. 22). But some Westerners feel, without denying the problems of an indefensible Uniatizing proselytism, that some Eastern Christians see some parts of the world as almost divinely determined to be Orthodox. Any encroachment by Westerners into this historically conditioned territory, even when it could conceivably assist the Orthodox to promote *aggiornamento*, is judged as condemnable even though they themselves have generally had freedom of evangelization in non-Orthodox settings!

The international consultations are not coterminous with the ecumenical work of Orthodox theology, but they do illustrate certain pitfalls that Ortho-

dox (as well as Catholics) face. The International
Consultation, in order to render visible its signifi-
cance, has asked for a proportionately large presence
of hierarchs besides the professional theologians and
church historians. This affords the potential of making the discussions especially sensitive to their pastoral implications, but it also means that a dispropor-
tionate amount of time is spent in ceremonial activities. Most regrettable has been the absence of Orthodox voices from the important churches of North
America.

Allow me to summarize several general com-
ments about the work of the International Commission. These ecumenical exchanges are notable in
character:

1) They include a large number of hierarchs and
not only professional theologians and church historians;

2) The number of languages to be accommo-
dated is considerable. Most of the drafting and
conceptualizing is done in French, with Greek and
English also having some importance, especially in
the final translations;

3) Several churches participating for the Orthodox are only recently beginning to emerge from
oppression under atheistic or non-Christian governments;

4) The awkwardness of having three preparatory groups meeting before each session of the
coordinating committee and hence the regular chal-

lenge to try to combine the fruits of three various drafting committees must be regretted;

5) The almost total absence of Orthodox voices from the important churches of North America until very recently is notable and regrettable;

6) The apparent decision to consider each text as a quasi definitive statement without willingness to rewrite and re-conceptualize the texts in the light of later critiques and suggestions is unfortunate, although the international commission has taken into consideration, in advance, suggestions from national dialogues such as the one in the USA;

7) The lack of proper dissemination of the agreed statements among the faithful of all the churches involved is regrettable.

These observations are not intended in any way to put-down the agreed statements or to question their usefulness. They are more an invitation to wider comprehensiveness. Every Christian committed to Church unity wants these conversations to flourish. We need to use every means at our disposal: prayer, good example, respect for other, and assiduous study to promote the success of this joint consultation.

The Fruits of the U.S. Joint National Consultation

I would like now to reflect briefly on the work of the United States Orthodox/Catholic Consultation which in the fall of 1995 celebrated its 50th meeting

here in Milwaukee. In 1970, when I returned to
North America from doctoral studies in Germany, I
was invited by the then Roman Catholic Bishop of
Worcester, Massachusetts, Bernard Flanagan, to
join the official bilateral consultation recently established by the National Conference of Catholic Bishops and the Standing Conference of Orthodox
Bishops of America (SCOBA) in order to promote
reconciliation between Orthodox and Catholics.
Since then, after my attending most of these fifty
theological consultations usually lasting three days,
as well as trips to Constantinople, Ukraine, Russia,
Greece, and lecturing in Rome's Pontifical Institute
for Eastern Christian Studies (Pontificio Instituto
Orientale), my understanding of my own church's
self-understanding and practice has been profoundly
enriched. I have also come to see that although
Rome officially considers itself as a sister church, it
sometimes acts like a bossy "big sister" or perhaps
even as an overly protective mother. I realized exis-
tentially that although the church of Rome is officially on record as being committed to living harmo-
niously with the Eastern churches, it does not do so
easily because of centuries of separation and its
unfortunate superiority complex.

In North America the Eastern churches have a
special opportunity to foster a unique understanding among churches. Here in this hemisphere ancient debates and animosities are not felt as intensely. Orthodox of different churches have a com-

mon language for discussion and enjoy an atmosphere of freedom from persecution by hostile governments that creates marvelous opportunities.

In the United States the official Orthodox/ Roman Catholic Consultation established in 1965 by the Standing Conference of Canonical Orthodox Bishops (SCOBA) and the National Conference of Catholic Bishops (NCCB) has followed with interest the work of the Joint International Commission. But it is also clear that the U.S. Consultation has accomplished more theological work than its international counterpart. The U. S. Consultation has followed a practice of responding jointly to the various agreed statements prepared by the International Commission.

Besides these responses to the International Consultation the United States Consultation has also published agreed statements on Eucharist, on mixed marriages, on respect for life, on the Church, on pastoral office, on the principle of *oikonomia* (accommodation), on the sanctity of marriage, on the spiritual formation of children from mixed marriages, and on the text of the Faith and Order Commission entitled *Baptism, Eucharist, and Ministry.*

In terms of published statements, the U.S. Orthodox/Roman Catholic documents have been modest in length and in frequency, especially when compared with the statements published by the Lutheran/Catholic and Anglican/Catholic dialogues. But in this particular consultation much preliminary work was necessary to overcome stereotypes and long-standing misconceptions. Other topics have been treated at the consultations so as to clarify theological views and canonical regulations. Among such topics have been the nature of ecumenical councils, the agenda of the future Pan-Orthodox Council, and the practical problems about the religious education of children in mixed marriages.

It is not possible here to summarize the American consensus statements, even though they are usually only short declarations, never more than two or three printed pages. What does emerge in these statements is repeated reference to "our remarkable and fundamental agreement" and "our common Christian tradition." It is true, one statement notes, that "our two traditions of viewing the Church are not easily harmonized. Yet we believe the Spirit is ever active to show us the way by which we can live together as one and many."

Sometimes the members of the American consultation knowing the upcoming agenda of the International Consultation would gently hint at perspectives to stress in the finished product. They also added neglected viewpoints. For instance, in its reaction to the New Valamo text on the sacrament of order, the American consultation in its "Apostolicity as God's Gift in the Life of the Church" stated that the concept of apostolicity needed to be broadened: "As an essential element in the life of the whole Church and of every Christian, apostolicity therefore is by no means unique to or limited to the realm of hierarchical ministry." (no. 9). The American response went on to say that "the apostolicity of ministry is generally seen as derived from the continuity of the community as a whole in apostolic life and faith" and that "apostolicity seems to consist more in fidelity to the apostles' proclamation and mission than in any one form of handing on community office." (no. 10).

Two recent texts from the American Consultation are worth noting especially. The first is a joint statement on "Tensions in Eastern Europe Related to 'Uniatism'" (May 28, 1992). The second is a statement of the Catholic members addressed to the Catholic community at large (October 31, 1992) which warns Roman Catholics, in light of post-Soviet disputes in formerly Communist dominated countries, that they may seem to be:

> …in danger of repeating yet again the same mistakes that in times past have deepened the estrangement between the Christian East and West. These mistakes consist principally in succumbing to two temptations. The first temptation for Catholics is to take action in Eastern Europe without respecting the ecclesial reality of the Orthodox churches. The vast material resources of the Catholic churches in the West mean that our actions will have an impact far greater than anything we can calculate beforehand. The second temptation is for the Catholic Church to treat the lands of Eastern Europe and the Middle East as "mission territory", that

is to day, for Catholics to feel that they must
simply turn Orthodox Christians, churches,
and cultures into Roman Catholic Christians,
churches, and cultures.

The text goes on to say that

What is needed now, however, is an unequivo-
cal assurance by Catholics that the Orthodox
churches will be treated as sister churches in
practice and not merely in theory, and that the
superior resources of the Catholic Church will
not be allowed to intimidate or seduce Orthodox Christians into abandoning their traditions. Such an assurance would be particularly
important regarding the situation of the many
"unchurched" people living in Eastern Europe
after decades of Communism. Our response as
Catholics to their plight ought to be to assist
Orthodox and Eastern Catholic communities
in their missions to these people. The "aid" that
Western Christians are sending into the Orthodox lands of Eastern Europe at this moment in
history must not become a cause of further
division between the Christian communities of
East and West.

Another fruit of the American consultation has
been the establishment in 1981 of a Joint Committee of Orthodox and Roman Catholic Bishops, the
only one of its kind in existence internationally.
This idea, first proposed by Fr. Nicon Patrinacos,
has led to a series to date of fourteen meetings the last
of which, from November 26 to December 6, 1995,
was held in Rome and then Constantinople.[18]

*Unresolved Tensions about
Eastern Catholic or "Uniate" Churches*

Despite the recent progress in mutual under-standing between the Churches of the East and West there still remain ignorance and prejudice among Catholics and Orthodox that must be eliminated by education and change of heart. Two areas in particu-lar threaten to undo much of the real progress that has been made in the past forty years. These areas relate to the existence of Eastern Catholic Churches which the Orthodox refer to as "Uniates" and to problems connected with what is perceived as proselytism.[19]

As a Roman Catholic it has taken me many years to begin to understand the basis for the griefs which the Orthodox have about "Uniates." I now under-stand that typically Orthodox, especially but not exclusively the Greek Orthodox, do not differenti-ate among Eastern Catholic churches the various occasions and historical contexts related to their emergence. The Greek Orthodox antipathy toward the creation "ex nihilo" of the Greek Catholic Church colors much of their perception of this question.

I judge it helpful especially for Catholics to hear the sharp tone of critique of Uniate churches that out of politeness is often not articulated at ecumeni-cal meetings. I take the following remarks made in 1970 as not untypical of the kind of Orthodox assessment of Uniates.

Uniate Churches were established mainly by exercise of civil power in cooperation with political factors and frequently by the exploitation of the unfavourable historical lot of certain Eastern peoples and their craving for national and religious independence and by ignoring the religious freedom and wishes of the (Orthodox) faithful themselves and most of their clergy. This could be the main explanation of the further fate of the Uniates, in some countries their growth and in others their liquidation. The occasional contribution made by Uniatism to the national, social, cultural and political development of certain regions in the East cannot offset the shadow it has cast and the negative effects it has had. Uniatism detached vital parts from the bodies of the various regional Eastern Churches and proved harmful to religious and national unity in the most crucial moments in the history of the people of certain Eastern countries. It cannot be justified merely on the ground that while changing its jurisdiction it preserved intact the faith of the particular Eastern churches and the Eastern rite in its liturgy. By changing its jurisdiction it brought about a separation between the hierarchy and the Christians in a particular district of the Church. By doing this, Uniatism rejected the rights of the local autocephalous church with its apostolic succession, diocesan immunity and historical justification, in favour of Roman Catholic jurisdiction, and to the detriment of ecumenism and love between the sister-churches. Uniatism contradicts the ecclesiology of the Roman Catholic Church itself and also runs counter to the principles of church government which have been established from ancient times."[20]

My purpose here is not to discuss the details of this Orthodox historical assessment. He probably underestimates the possibility that in some settings individual Orthodox churches may have legitimately desired to enter into full visible communion with Rome because of their convictions about the importance of the Church of Rome. I cite that passage to illustrate simply the intensity of Orthodox sensitivity on this matter which is still very much alive.

Some of the Orthodox difficulties with Eastern Catholicism are rooted in what they, as well as some Catholics, see as tensions inherent in the two different ecclesiologies enshrined in two separate Vatican II documents: the Decree on Ecumenism (*Unitatis Redintegratio*) and the Dogmatic Constitution on the Church (*Lumen gentium*). They cannot unify what these two council texts say about the Eastern Catholic Churches and Orthodoxy. Is it not inconsistent to regard the Eastern Catholic Churches as "bridge churches" between the East and the West as they are in the Ecumenism decree if the Orthodox Churches are described in *Lumen gentium* as "sister churches"? In the eventuality of official recognition of full visible communion between Orthodoxy and Roman Catholicism the question is asked what would then be the "home" of the Eastern Catholics? Would they retain their own autonomy or would they perhaps seek appropriate bonds of unity with their Orthodox Eastern counterpart especially in those more frequent situations where they were originally members of the Orthodox Church?

Orthodox and Catholics alike have noted that texts of Vatican II fail to mention the often troubled history of the relationship between the Eastern and Western Churches. The Orthodox have objected that there is no allusion to disedifying incidents regarding Rome's interference in the affairs of the Eastern churches, although, as we have noted, there is a discreet reference (no. 7) in connection with the text of 1 Jn 1:10 ("If we say that we have not sinned"...) to sins against unity. What were these sins? The Roman church often displayed arrogance and intolerance, hunger for power, racism, and religious imperialism reflected in pushing Latinization upon these churches, often downgrading the authentic traditions of the churches of the East, and engaging in sharp polemics with their Orthodox mother churches.

The Future

I have attempted through this overview of the emergence of the concept "sister churches," of the international and national official dialogues underway between churches of the East and West, and of problems relating to "Uniatism" and proselytism, to invite us all to rethink profoundly our understanding of the relationship between the churches of

Rome and Byzantium. It is one thing to speak glowingly about sister churches and to proclaim that the Church of Christ subsists not only in the church of Rome but in the other churches as well, but quite another thing to adapt our practices to coincide with that those affirmations. This century has certainly witnessed dramatic symbolic and diplomatic gestures between East and West. What is needed now is action on the dogmatic and canonical front: formal recognition of each other in such a way that Orthodoxy would not be required to accept as binding all the decisions formulated in general councils of the West including Trent and Vatican I as well as the promulgations of the papacy in 1854 and 1950.[21] Have we given up completely on trying to re-establish eucharistic sharing between our two churches? What needs to be done doctrinally and canonically before this could take place officially? What hinders truly evangelical, gospel-like witnessing is our unwillingness to admit, not just theoretically, the ecclesial nature of the other church and to recognize formally its baptisms, eucharists, and ordinations. The decline in candidates for presbyteral ordination in the Roman church has also led to a decline in well trained priest-theologians to collaborate with the lay theologians (whose top priority is only rarely research into the historical and doctrinal causes of estrangement between Christian East and West). It would be a tragedy indeed if all the promising efforts and labors of this century's church leaders and theologians for restoring full communion are not concretely realized.

At the University of Toronto, I offer a course entitled: "Eastern Christian Contributions to the Churches of the West." Such a course responds to a request by Vatican II and later by a Prefect of the Vatican Congregation for Christian Education, William Cardinal Baum, who on January 6, 1987 urged Latin Catholics, especially its future priests, to study seriously the heritages of the Eastern churches so as to respect their rights. Continuing education programs on the uniqueness of the churches of the Christian East would be helpful even for members of various Vatican curial offices. I do not ignore the measure of strained tension that often exists between the churches of Rome and of the East; I would argue however that this is not because of ill will but rather by often shocking unfamiliarity with the traditions of the East.

Other important events have taken place in recent years such as the publication of the *Code of Canons of the Eastern Churches* promulgated on October 18, 1990.

This year, 1996, there may well be organized celebrations designed to commemorate the 400th anniversary of the Union of Brest (1596). This commemoration will have to be organized with special attention to the promises made by Rome at that time and also the particularity (*sui juris* character) of the Ukrainian Catholic Church within the Catholic communion.

What Specific Actions are Needed?

Catholics can promote an improvement in dealings between the church of Rome and the Eastern churches not in full visible communion with it by a number of actions.

Here I suggest five means. (1) Our lives need to reflect Gospel values; (2) we need to promote the virtue of boldness (*parresia*); (3) we must promote solid historical and theological scholarship; (4) we must learn to contextualize and interpret documents of the papacy and Vatican curia; and (5) need to continue to express visibly the ties of communion already existing with our sister churches of Orthodoxy.

1. Let our lives reflect Gospel values. The Christian's primary vocation is obviously to become living witnesses to the values and truths of the Gospel. All our successes in achieving smooth and efficient governance between center and periphery would mean little if they are not accompanied by growth in Christian living. I do not mean this in a pietistic or sentimental way, and I do not imply that the East needs this challenge more than the West. But we need to enter into the "mysteries" of revelation, contemplating the wonder of the Incarnation, seeing the present-day world bathed in the power of the Risen Christ, communicating—through our reverence for icons and through the divine liturgy—with the heavenly church to which we are called. The

transforming power of lived Christianity will give a
ringing note of authenticity to our demands for
structural change.

In his book *The Shape of the Church to Come*,
whose German title was *Structural Change in the
Church*, the late Roman Catholic theologian Karl
Rahner made a point that illustrates what I am
talking about. Using the example of a chess club, he
asked: Who are the most important members of
such a club? Its president, vice-president, treasurer,
or secretary? Or are the most important members
not the best chess-players? Christian make an incal-
culable contribution to the reform of church polity,
if they themselves are transformed by the Gospel.
There should be a sense of excitement in our convictions about Christianity that is contagious.

2. My second suggestion is for us to promote the
rare virtue which the New Testament calls boldness
or free expression (*parresia*) and extols in Acts 2:29
and 4:13. In an imperfect and sinful church it is a
necessary virtue for conducting ourselves appropri-
ately. One of my former professors, Joseph Cardinal
Ratzinger, before he became increasingly concerned
about the danger of "confusing the simple," wrote
eloquently about the need for this virtue of boldness
or prophetic utterance. Let me quote his own words:

> The servility of the sycophants (branded by the
> genuine prophets of the Old Testament as 'false
> prophets'), of those who shy from and shun
> every collision, who prize above all their calm

complacency, is not true obedience... What the church needs today as always, are not adulators to extol the status quo, but persons whose humility and obedience are not less than their passion for truth; persons who brace every mis-understanding and attack, as they bear witness; persons who, in a word, love the church more than ease and the unruffled course of their personal destiny.[22]

I can not imagine a more eloquent formulation of "tough love" for the church than this description by the early Ratzinger. He explains why we occasion-ally have to protest and represent our contrary judgments or opinions. This is difficult when the very people whose decisions are being questioned consider this boldness not as a virtue but as disloyal dissent. The church can not move ahead in reform unless we convince those persons that there is a reputable form of disagreement, which is basically loyal opposition to specific prudential judgments made most likely without sufficient consultation.

3. We also need of course to promote solid historical and theological scholarship. That the Ref-ormation of the 16th century began at a university is not surprising. The power of ideas, the probative impact of critical and serious historical research, can never be underestimated in the church. The church needs not only the official authoritative magisterium vested in the hierarchy, but also that complementary magisterium of the magisters: theologians and other scholars such as church historians. The Latin term

magisterium especially since the 19th century has come to mean that special group of persons known as hierarchs, whereas it originally meant "teaching activity," a ministry undertaken at many levels within the church.

4. Next there is need to contextualize documents coming from the papacy and the Vatican Curia. We need to appreciate that the Vatican officials are convinced that many ordinary believers are thoroughly confused and even disedified by the speculations of theologians and pastoral care givers. These officials judge that true discernment among churchgoers is clouded by pervasive consumerism and materialism. They are slow to recognize a directive may contain in part subtle but real forms of cultural imperialism, based on prejudices of Western Europe. In their desire for unity in the Church, these officials often end up arguing for uniformity. Not only the East but the West too judges punitive actions taken against maverick theologians or bishops as excessive. The East will be very sensitive to any measures taken by Rome to limit the authority of national episcopal conferences since this is one of the expressions of synodality central to the life of Eastern churches or to punitive actions taken against theologians that seem to lack due process. Here both East and West wish for limited intervention by the Vatican curia.[23]

5. Finally, my suggestion is for all of us to express visibly the ties of communion with the sister

churches of Orthodoxy. Because of the burden of past history and recent painful actions by governments and churches, there exists among Christians, especially in Eastern Europe, a high degree of resentment, antipathy, suspicion, and even fear of other Christian churches. If such attitudes are to be overcome, it is essential that churches of the East and West together formulate and implement practical recommendations. Mutual consultation by Catholics and Orthodox at all levels, particularly before any activities are undertaken which might even inadvertently give offense to others, is crucial. In countries previously under Communist oppression, a healthy interaction between the Orthodox church and the Roman church or even between the Orthodox church and the Eastern Catholic church could lead to important developments in theological renewal, liturgical reform, and useful formulation of Christian social and political doctrine.

How will the Catholic churches remain faithful to their deepest religious heritage and at the same time enrich the church of Rome and other Western Christian communities? This will be done by their helping believers understand better Eastern church life. This will stress the importance of the local church where the faithful come together as church in one place (1 Cor 11:17, 20; 14:23, 26), becoming the body of Christ in the eucharist. The bishop will be seen as acting to represent the local church and to govern more widely in synodal fashion. A typical

Eastern perspective is that the eucharistic assembly under the presidency of the bishop is completely church in all its fullness, a complete church even if not the total church. The church that dwells in Milwaukee or Stamford has the same fullness as the church in Rome, Melbourne, or Buenos Aires. This implies the basic unity and equality of all local churches and of all bishops which does not mean uniformity, just as the unity of essence in the triune God does not exclude plurality among the unique persons. Among the churches some may be called upon to "preside in love." Many factors contribute to a church's potential for presiding: antiquity, presumed apostolicity of foundation, martyrdoms, geopolitical advantages, size, or wealth.

The church of Rome would profit from the experience of the Eastern churches regarding the role of particular churches, the synodal structure of government, the ways of expressing unity amid diversity, the healing power of the Divine Liturgy for resolving even ethnic tensions. In the United States and Canada, the Eastern churches have a special opportunity to foster a unique understanding among churches. In our hemisphere, ancient debates and animosities are not felt as intensely. Orthodox and Catholics are in a better position to dialogue because here they have enjoyed freedom from years of persecution by hostile, officially atheistic governments. The Roman church will be enriched through the East's love of liturgy, its rich prayer traditions, its love of the Fathers, its devotion to icons, its creative church structures, and its ability to heal nationalistic antagonisms through prayer and charity. All of us must continue to work together to fulfil that dream.

I do not want to be heard as a prophet of doom. If I sound critical, it is because I am emboldened by my concern that workers for the Christian East are fast becoming an aging minority dying out, in need of replacement. In no way do I minimize the achievements, sometimes amazing, of the past and present, often in the face of hardships. But we need to plan for the future imaginatively if we are not to witness another missed opportunity in the life of our churches. Despite the recent progress in mutual understanding between the churches of the East and West there still remains much ignorance and prejudice that needs to be overcome by proper education and change of heart.

The many theologians and historians who have belonged to this ongoing dialogue have embodied a profound commitment to healing the divisions between our two sister churches. They have worked under difficult circumstances since all of the Consultation members are heavily burdened with academic, pastoral and administrative duties. The number of available Orthodox theologians for this task is limited; the same persons are called upon their church leaders to assume multiple ecumenical responsibilities. The number of Catholic historians and theologians who understand the traditions and experiences of the East is also, despite our size, rather circumscribed. To those who criticize the lateness of our position papers, the insufficiencies of our footnotes, the brevity of our statements, the late of dissemination of our research, we plead overcommitment not laziness.

The role of the co-presiders, not only at the meetings, but in the behind-the-scenes negotiations, has been notable. This leadership and ministry of oversight illustrates tellingly what our churches understand by the responsibilities of those called upon to exercise *episkope.* If the theologians have been busy and overworked, the same applies to our presiding bishops.

One of the critical tasks that we have perhaps neglected is the formation and preparation of young scholars to continue our work. The present membership must soon hand over the unfinished tasks to new and younger persons. We have not interacted satisfactorily with our seminaries and departments of theology to discover new talent and encourage specific forms of research.

We have not listened sufficiently to the faithful at large in our churches and learned from their experiences and insights. On the few occasions when they have interacted with us, and not just by singing in our choirs, preparing our meals, or chauffeuring us to and fro, we have heard words of wisdom that do not get reflected in our minutes and agendas. For them we need the gift of ears!

Our much vaunted desire for sharing our conclusions with churchgoers in both communions has yet to be realized. Can we not find ways to "popularize" for the faithful what we have come to realize about our common history and teachings?

These and other desiderata dominate as they must the agenda for the years leading up to A.D. 2000 and beyond.

Endnotes

[1] See Ronald G. Roberson, *The Eastern Christian Churches: A Brief Survey.* 3rd rev. ed. (Rome: Pontifical Oriental Institute, 1990). For a more complete but easily accessible account of the Eastern churches by a Roman Catholic see Aidan Nichols, O.P., *Rome and the Eastern Churches: A Study in Schism* (Collegeville: Liturgical Press, 1992). See also the helpful exposition by a Greek Orthodox theologian: Thomas E. FitzGerald, *The Orthodox Church*, Denominations in America no. 7 (Westport, CT: Greenwood, 1995). An older work, but still useful, is Edward J. Kilmartin, S.J., *Toward Reunion: The Roman Catholic and the Orthodox Churches* (New York: Paulist, 1979).

[2] Congar's book commemorating the 900th anniversary of the mutual anathemas of A.D. 1054 was published in English as *After Nine Hundred Years: The Background of the Schism between the Eastern and Western Churches* (New York: Fordham University, 1959). It was originally published as part of the two-volume work *L'Eglise et les églises. 1054-1954. Neuf siècles de douloureuse séparation entre l'Orient et l'Occident. Etudes et travaux sur l'unité chrétienne offerts à Dom Lambert Beauduin* (Chevetogne: Editions de Chevetogne, 1954-55).

[3] See Michael Fahey, "Twentieth Century Shifts in Roman Catholic Attitudes toward Ecumenism," in *Catholic Perspectives on Baptism, Eucharist, and Ministry* (Lanham, MD: University Press of America, 1986), pp. 27-43.

[4] Constantin G. Patelos, ed., *The Orthodox Church in the Ecumenical Movement (1902-75)* (Geneva: World Council of Churches, 1978; D. Papandreou and P. Duprey, et al., edd.s *Tomos Agapis: Vatican-Phanar (1958-1970)* (Rome: Imprimerie Polyglotte Vaticane, 1971), translated and expanded to the year 1984 by E.J. Stormon, S.J., *Towards the Healing of Schism: The Sees of Rome and Constantinople* (New York: Paulist, 1987). A recent update is found in *Orthodox*

Visions of Ecumenism: Statements, Messages and Reports of the Ecumenical Movement 1902-1992, ed. Gennadios Limouris (Geneva: World Council of Churches, 1994). See also O. S. Tomkins, "The Roman Catholic Church and the Ecumenical Movement 1910-1948," in R. Rouse and S. C. Neill, ed., *A History of the Ecumenical Movement 1517-1948* (rev. ed.; Philadelphia: Westminster, 1967), pp. 675-693; Georges Florovsky, "The Orthodox Churches and the Ecumenical Movement Prior to 1910," *ibid.*, pp. 171-215; and Nicolas Zernov, "The Eastern Churches and the Ecumenical Movement in the Twentieth Century," *ibid.*, pp. 645-674. See also, Michael A. Fahey, S.J., "Orthodox Ecumenism and Theology: 1970-1983," *Theological Studies* 39 (1978) 446-485; 44 (1983) 625-692.

[5] Citations to the texts of Vatican II are given throughout from the translation edited by Norman P. Tanner, S.J., *Decrees of the Ecumenical Councils*, Vol. 2: *Trent to Vatican II* (Washington: Georgetown University; London: Sheed and Ward, 1990).

[6] Emmanuel Lanne, O.S.B., "Églises unies ou églises soeurs: Un choix inéluctable," *Irénikon* 48 (1975) 322-42; English: "United Churches or Sister Churches: A Choice to be Faced," *One in Christ* 12 (1976) 106-23. See also his "Eglises-soeurs: Implications ecclésiologiques du Tomos Agapis," *Istina* 20 (1975) 47-74 and his "Église soeur et église mère dans le vocabulaire de l'église ancienne," in *Communio sanctorum: Mélanges offerts à Jean-Jacques von Allmen* (Geneva: Labor et Fides, 1982). John Meyendorff also published an important study with the same title as Lanne's essay in *Istina* 20 (1975) 35-46. This material was summarized at length and analyzed by Bishop Maximos [Aghiorgoussis] in an unpublished text presented at the U.S. Orthodox/Catholic consultation on May 14, 1993.

[7] Michael A. Fahey, S.J., "*Ecclesiae Sorores ac Fratres*: Sibling Communion in the Pre-Nicene Christian Era," *Catholic Theological Society of America: Proceedings* 36 (1981) 15-38.

[8] Yves Congar, "Église orthodoxe et église catholique romaine: 'Églises-soeurs' et conciles 'oecuméniques'," in his *Diversités et communion* (Paris: Cerf, 1982) 126-41.

[9] The full text is in AAS 62 (1970) 753. See also *Documents on Anglican/Roman Catholic Relations, I* (Washington: USCC, 1972), pp. 42-43.

[10] The Society for the Law of the Oriental Churches (an ecumenical association including Oriental, Orthodox, Catholic and Protestant members) held its fourth congress in 1978 in Regensburg on the theme: "The Church and the Churches—Autonomy and Autocephaly." The communications given at the meeting have been published in two volumes as: *Die Kirche und die Kirchen: Autonomie und Autokephalie*, Kanon, Bd. IV and V (Vienna: Wissenschaftliche Gesellschaft Oesterreichs, 1980). For a Catholic critique of the Western Catholic two-tier structure, see George Nedungatt, S.J., "Autonomy, Autocephaly, and the Problem of Jurisdiction Today," Bd. V, pp. 19-35. See also, Hervé Legrand, "La réalisation de l'Église en un lieu," in *Initiation à la pratique de la théologie*, edd. B. Lauret and F. Refoulé, Vol. 3/2 (Paris: Cerf, 1983) pp. 143-345.

[11] The late Orthodox theologian John Meyendorff (1926-1992), at a 1980 symposium in Bologna, noted the dangerous evolution of legitimate canonical regionalism in the East into ecclesiastical nationalism and a factor of division. See: "Régionalisme ecclésiastique, structures de communion ou couverture de séparatisme?" in *Les Églises après Vatican II: Dynamisme et prospective*, ed. G. Alberigo, Théologie historique 61 (Paris: Beauchesne, 1981), pp. 329-345; English text: "Ecclesiastical Regionalism: Structures of Communion or Cover for Separatism?" in his *The Byzantine Legacy in the Orthodox Church* (Crestwood, NY: St. Vladimir's Seminary Press, 1982), pp. 217-233.

[12] See Adolf Lumpe, "Zur Geschichte der Wörter *Concilium* und *Synodus* in der Antiken Christlichen Latinität," *Annuarium Historiae Conciliorum* 2 (1970) 1-21; "Zur

Geschichte des Wortes Synodus in der antiken Gräzität," *Annuarium Historiae Conciliorum* 6 (1974) 40-53. See also, Gustav Koffmane, *Geschichte des Kirchenlateins*, Vol. I (Breslau: 1879) 27 ff.

[13] See, Günther Stemberger, "Stammt das synodale Element der Kirche aus der Synagoge?" *Annuarium Historiae Conciliorum* 8 (1976) 1-14. This volume of the *Annuarium* was published under the title *Synodale Strukturen der Kirche: Entwicklung und Probleme*, ed. W. Brandmüller (Donauworth: Auer, 1977).

[14] *Theology and the Church*, trans. by Robert Barringer (Crestwood: St. Vladimir's, 1980) 56-57.

[15] "The Institution of Episcopal Conferences: An Orthodox Reflection," in *The Nature and Future of Episcopal Conferences*, ed. H. Legrand et al. (Washington: Catholic University of America, 1988), pp. 376-383. On the ecclesiology of Zizioulas, see: Gaëtan Baillargeon, *Perspectives orthodoxes sur l'Église-Communion: L'oeuvre de Jean Zizioulas* (Montreal: Editions Paulines, 1989) and Paul McPartlan, *The Eucharist Makes the Church: Henri de Lubac and John Zizioulas in Dialogue* (Edinburgh: T. & T. Clark, 1993).

[16] See Michael A. Fahey, "Eastern Synodal Traditions: Pertinence for Western Collegial Institutions," in: Thomas J. Reese, ed., *Episcopal Conferences: Historical, Canonical, Theological Studies* (Washington: Georgetown University, 1989) 253-65. Also, Pierre Duprey, "La structure synodale de l'église dans la théologie orientale," *Proche orient chrétien* 20 (1970) 123-45, English: "The Synodical Structure of the Church in Eastern Theology," *One in Christ* 7 (1971) 152-82; U. Mosiek, "Der Bischofssynode der lateinischen Kirche und die ständige Synode der unierten Kirchen," *Ex aequo et bono: Willibald M. Plöchl zum 70. Geburtstag*, ed. P. Leisching (Innsbruck: Wagner, 1977); Stanley Harakas, "The Local Church: An Eastern Orthodox Perspective," *Ecumenical Review* 29 (1977) 141-53; Heinrich Fries, "Synoden und Konzilien im Leben der Kirche: Historisch-systematische

Aspekte," *Catholica* 34 (1980) 174-193; Michael Kessler, "Das synodale Prinzip: Bemerkungen zu seiner Entwicklung und Bedeutung," *Theologische Quartalschrift* 168 (1988) 43-60.

[17] For a complete selection of the international and national (USA) statements see: *Orthodox and Catholics in Dialogue: Documents of the Joint International Commission and Official Documents in the United States 1965-1995*, ed. John Borelli and John Erickson (Washington: USCC; Crestwood, NY: St. Vladimir's Seminary Press, 1996). The international texts (with a commentary) have been published by Paul McPartlan, ed., *One in 2000? Towards Catholic-Orthodox Unity* (Middlegreen, Slough: St. Pauls, 1993). The international texts have also appeared separately in *Origins*. See: "The Mystery of the Church and of the Eucharist in the Light of the Mystery of the Holy Trinity," [Munich document, July 6, 1982] in: *Origins* 12 (August 12, 1982) 157-160; (cf. US Orthodox/Catholic response May 25, 1983 in *Origins* 13 (August 4, 1983) 167); "Faith, Sacraments and the Unity of the Church," [Bari document, August 1, 1987] in: *Origins* 17 (April 14, 1988) 743-749; (cf. US Orthodox/Catholic response June 2, 1988); "The Sacrament of Order in the Sacramental Structure of the Church with Particular Reference to the Importance of Apostolic Succession for the Sanctification and Unity of the People of God," [New Valamo document, June 26, 1988] in *Origins* 18 (October 13, 1988) 297-300; (cf. US Orthodox/ Catholic response, October 26-28, 1989); "Uniatism, Method of Union of the Past, and the Present Search for Full Communion [Balamand document June 23, 1993] in *Origins* 23 (August 12, 1993) 166-169; (cf. US Orthodox/Catholic response October 15, 1994, in *Origins* 24 (February 9, 1995) 570-572. See also the statements of the US Orthodox/Catholic Consultation of November 1, 1986, submitted to the Joint International Commission entitled: "Apostolicity as God's Gift in the Life of the Church" as well as "Primacy and Conciliarity," dated

October 26-28, 1990 printed in *Origins* 19 (December 21, 1989) 469-472. Some of these texts appear also in *Building Unity*, Ecumenical Documents IV, ed. Joseph A. Burgess and Jeffrey Gros (New York: Paulist, 1989) and *Growing Consensus: U.S. 1962-1991*, Ecumenical Documents V, ed. Joseph A. Burgess and Jeffrey Gros (New York: Paulist, 1995).

[18] The dates of these Bishops' meetings have been: Sept. 30-Oct. 1, 1981 (New York City); Oct. 6-7, 1982 (Milwaukee); Oct. 6-7, 1983 (New York City); Sept. 20-21, 1984 (Morristown, NJ); Sept. 10-11, 1986 (Tuxedo Park, NY); Nov. 10-11, 1987 (Milwaukee); Sept. 6-8, 1988 (Boston); Oct. 3-5, 1989 (Gulf Shores, Alabama); Oct. 3-5, 1990 (Johnstown, PA); Sept. 17-19, 1991 (Baltimore, MD); Sept. 30—Oct. 2, 1992 (Tenafly, NJ); Mar. 8-9, 1994 (Detroit); Oct. 4-6, 1994 (Pittsburgh). The visits to the Vatican and the Phanar took place from Nov. 26 to Dec. 6, 1995. The Bishops have produced four agreed statements of their own regarding: Ordination (1988); Marriage (1990); Eastern Europe [I] (1991); and Eastern Europe [II] (1992). These texts are published in the Borelli and Erickson book cited above.

[19] For a short but incisive account of this situation see Rembert G. Weakland, "Crisis in Orthodox-Catholic Relations: Challenges and Hopes," *America* 166 (January 25, 1992) 30-35.

[20] Ivan Panchovski and Todor Sabev, "An Orthodox Comment [regarding the 1970 Joint Working Group Study Document "Common Witness and Proselytism"]," *Ecumenical Review* 23 (1971) 27-28.

[21] Yves Congar has argued for a *hierarchia conciliorum*. In the event of establishing full communion with the See of Rome, Orthodoxy would not be asked to accept the Western medieval councils as "ecumenical" but only as legitimate general councils of the West. As such, these councils would be seen as addressing specifically Western concerns, and for

the Orthodox the canons of Trent or Vatican I, for example, would not per se have absolutely binding force. See also Joseph Ratzinger, "Rome and the Churches of the East after the Removal of the Ban of Excommunication of 1054," in his *Principles of Catholic Theology: Building Stones for a Fundamental Theology*, trans. Sister Mary Frances McCarthy (San Francisco: Ignatius, 1987), pp. 203-218.

22 Joseph Ratzinger, "Free Expression and Obedience in the Church," in *The Church: Readings in Theology* (New York: Kenedy, 1963), pp. 194-217, here 212 and 215.

23 Peter Huizing and Knut Walf, *The Roman Curia and the Communion of Churches* (*Concilium* 127; New York: Seabury, 1979); and Brian Daley, "Structures of Charity: Bishops' Gatherings and the See of Rome in the Early Church," in *Episcopal Conferences: Historical, Canonical and Theological Studies*, pp. 25-58.

THE PÈRE MARQUETTE LECTURES IN THEOLOGY

Marquette University

1975 *The Contributions of Theology to Medical Ethics*
James Gustafson
University Professor of Theological Ethics
University of Chicago

1976 *Religious Values in an Age of Violence*
Rabbi Marc Tannenbaum
Director of National Interreligious Affairs
American Jewish Committee, New York City

1977 *Truth Beyond Relativism:*
Karl Mannheim's Sociology of Knowledge
Gregory Baum
Professor of Theology and Religious Studies
St. Michael's College

1978 *A Theology of 'Uncreated Energies'*
George A. Maloney, S.J.
Professor of Theology
John XXIII Center for Eastern Christian
Studies
Fordham University

1980 *Method in Theology:*
An Organon For Our Time
Frederick E. Crowe, S.J.
Research Professor in Theology
Regis College, Toronto

1981 *Catholics in the Promised Land of the Saints*
James Hennesey, S.J.
Professor of the History of Christianity
Boston College

Marquette University

1987 *Nova et Vetera:*
  The Theology of Tradition in American Catholicism
    Gerald Fogarty
    Professor of Religious Studies
    University of Virginia

1988 *The Christian Understanding of Freedom and the*
  History of Freedom in the Modern Era:
  The Meeting and Confrontation Between
  Christianity and the Modern Era in a Postmodern
  Situation
    Walter Kasper
    Professor of Dogmatic Theology
    University of Tübingen

1989 *Moral Absolutes: Catholic Tradition, Current*
  Trends, and the Truth
    William F. May
    Ordinary Professor of Moral Theology
    Catholic University of America

1990 *Is Mark's Gospel a Life of Jesus? The Question of*
  Genre
    Adela Yarbro Collins
    Professor of New Testament
    University of Notre Dame

1991 *Faith, History and Cultures:*
  Stability and Change in Church Teachings
    Walter H. Principe, C.S.B.
    Professor of Theology
    University of Toronto

About the Père Marquette Lecture Series

The Annual Père Marquette Lecture Series began at Marquette University in the Spring of 1969. Ideal for classroom use, library additions, or private collections, the Père Marquette Lecture Series has received international acceptance by scholars, universities, and libraries. Hardbound in blue cloth with gold stamped covers. Uniform style and price ($15 each). Some reprints with soft covers. Complete set (26 Titles) receives a 40% discount. New standing orders receive a 30% discount. Regular reprinting keeps all volumes available. Ordering information (purchase orders, checks, and major credit cards accepted):

Bookmasters Distribution Services
1444 U.S. Route 42
Mansfield OH 44903
Order Toll-Free (800) 247-6553
FAX: (419) 281 6883

Editorial Address:
Dr. Andrew Tallon, Director
Marquette University Press
Box 1881
Milwaukee WI 53201-1881
Tel: (414) 288-7298
FAX: (414) 288-3300
Internet: tallona@vms.csd.mu.edu
CompuServe : 73627,1125.

ISBN 0-87462-576-9